# Dolphins

by Morgan Lloyd

PEARSON

Scott
Foresman

Editorial Offices: Glenview, Illinois • Parsippany, New Jersey • New York, New York
Sales Offices: Needham, Massachusetts • Duluth, Georgia • Glenview, Illinois
Coppell, Texas • Ontario, California • Mesa, Arizona

**Dolphins** belong to a group of animals called mammals. Similar to other mammals, dolphins are warm-blooded. They live underwater, but they have lungs and breathe air. They must come to the **surface** to breathe.

Unlike fish, dolphins do not hatch from eggs. They are born live and drink milk from their mothers. When they are born, they have whiskerlike hairs on their snouts. Most dolphins lose these hairs soon after birth.

There are more than thirty different kinds of dolphins. They live in every ocean in the world, from Arctic seas to tropical waters. They can be found both near to and far from shore. Although there are many kinds of dolphins, they all have some body parts in common.

The flaps on a dolphin's tail are called flukes. The flukes and tail provide the power to help dolphins swim and leap through the water. The flippers are also called pectoral fins. They help a dolphin steer.

**Dorsal fin**

**Fluke**

All dolphins have blowholes at the top of their heads. This is how they take in air. The mouth of a dolphin is called its beak. The shape of the beak can vary greatly among different kinds of dolphins.

Under their thick, **flexible** skin, dolphins have a layer of fat called blubber. The blubber helps keep them warm in the cold ocean waters.

The number of teeth a dolphin has varies, but all dolphin teeth are cone-shaped.

Jawbone with teeth

Blowhole

Beak

Pectoral fin (flipper)

# Dolphin Communication

Dolphins are amazing communicators. They make several kinds of sounds. They can make whistling and clicking noises. They can even make sounds that resemble chirps, yelps, and squeaks.

Many dolphins have their own special whistles. As dolphins travel together in groups, they may repeat their own whistles from time to time. These signature whistles may help dolphins know who is around them. After a baby dolphin is born, the mother may whistle to the baby for several days almost without stopping. This helps the baby dolphin learn its mother's whistle.

# Bowriding

Dolphins are often seen riding the waves in front of boats. This is called bowriding. When dolphins bowride, they get an extra push from the water in front of the boat. This extra push from the water allows them to glide along, rising to the surface when they need to breathe. By traveling this way, they use less energy.

## Bottle-nosed Dolphin

The bottle-nosed dolphin is one of the best-known dolphins. It is found in coastal waters around the world. The bottle-nosed dolphin gets its name from the shape of its beak. The beak is usually about three inches long. The size of the bottle-nosed dolphin varies from about six-and-one-half feet to nearly thirteen feet long. These dolphins often travel in groups of five to one hundred members.

Some bottle-nosed dolphins can be trained to perform.

Bottle-nosed dolphins can vary quite a bit in color, but they usually have light gray upper bodies with pinkish gray bellies.

You can often see bottle-nosed dolphins at an **aquarium** because of their intelligence and trainability. Aquarium dolphins may perform tricks for an audience. The bottle-nosed dolphin can leap as high as twenty feet into the air.

## Common Dolphin

Common dolphins can be recognized by the yellowish patches on their sides. They are often seen in groups of more than one hundred and sometimes as many as two thousand! They are very active at the surface. It is not unusual to catch **glimpses** of these ocean acrobats as they leap, somersault, or ride the waves in front of boats.

Like other kinds of dolphins, common dolphins often work together in large groups to hunt fish. When they find a school of fish, they spread out and make a circle, forcing the fish into the middle. Then the dolphins take turns feeding.

## Hourglass Dolphin

The hourglass dolphin's sharp black-and-white coloring makes it easy to recognize. It is only found in the cold waters surrounding Antarctica. At about six feet long, it is somewhat smaller than other dolphins. Its black beak is so short that it might not be noticed.

Hourglass dolphins travel in much smaller groups than other dolphins. There may be as few as two or as many as forty hourglass dolphins swimming together. Like other dolphins, they leap in the air and ride the waves in front of boats.

## Amazon River Dolphin

The Amazon River dolphin lives in the Amazon River in South America. It is about eight feet long. The Amazon River dolphin usually swims alone or with one other partner.

This freshwater dolphin is usually pink! Babies are born a light gray color, but they become more pink as they grow. The Amazon River dolphin has a ridge along its back instead of a fin. Its flippers are longer than those of most dolphins.

The Amazon River dolphin cannot see as well as other dolphins. It makes **pulses** of sound that bounce off underwater objects. This echo helps the dolphin get around and find food. It also has whiskerlike hairs on its beak. These whiskers may help it feel for food on the murky river bottom.

## Risso's Dolphin

The Risso's dolphin has an unusual shape. Its head is large and blunt, and it has no beak. Its dark-gray body is often covered with scars, which can make it look almost white. The scars come from tooth marks made by other Risso's dolphins.

These dolphins are quite large. They can be about ten to thirteen feet long.

The Risso's dolphin is found in deeper waters, far from shore. It eats mostly octopuses and squid.

## Enchanted Creatures

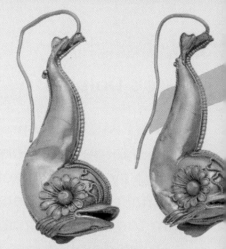

For hundreds of years, people have imagined that dolphins are **enchanted** creatures. The playful mammals appear in artwork that is thousands of years old. People have also created jewelry to look like dolphins. Sailors

These dolphin-shaped earrings are from ancient Rome.

enjoyed seeing dolphins playing in the water by their ships. They believed the dolphins brought good fortune, or luck.

Dolphins are even part of mythology. The Greek god of the sea, Poseidon, was sometimes said to ride a chariot pulled by dolphins. Other stories say that dolphins came to the rescue of shipwrecked sailors and lost fishermen. The dolphin also has a constellation named in its honor. This constellation is called Delphinius.

Despite the differences among species, dolphins have much in common. Dolphins have amazing skills, characteristics, and even talents. They have also been recognized throughout history in different ways. These marine mammals interact playfully and intelligently with each other and their environments. They are important members of aquatic life. Dolphins are unique and special creatures.

This dolphin-shaped oil container is from ancient Greece.

# Glossary

aquarium *n.* a building used for showing collections of live fish, water animals, and water plants.

dolphins *n.* sea mammals related to the whale, but smaller.

enchanted *adj.* delightful, charming.

flexible *adj.* easily bent, not stiff.

glimpses *n.* short, quick viewings or looks.

pulses *n.* regular, measured beats.

surface *n.* the top layer.